101 DISTINCTIONS
between
SUCCESS and FAILURE

KEITH CAMERON SMITH
and
DOUG HANSON

WKU Publishing

Published by WKU Publishing
www.keithcameronsmith.com

PUBLISHER'S CATALOGING-IN-PUBLICATION DATA
Smith, Keith Cameron.
  101 distinctions between success and failure / Keith Cameron Smith and Doug Hanson — Ormond Beach, Florida : WKU Publishing, 2007.

  p. ; cm.
  ISBN-13: 978-0-9755070-2-5

  1. Success. 2. Failure (Psychology). 3. Self-realization.
I. Hanson, Doug. II. Title.

BF637 .S8 S55 2006   2006927165
158.1—dc22   0607

Printed in the United States of America
10   9   8   7   6   5   4   3

Design by To The Point Solutions
www.tothepointsolutions.com

101 DISTINCTIONS
between
SUCCESS and FAILURE

CONTENTS

ACKNOWLEDGEMENTS

To my wife and best friend, thank you for your love and support. You are truly an angel and an awesome mom. To my children, I love being your daddy! To my parents, you gave me roots and wings and have been a great example of love. To my many mentors who have become my friends, especially Nido Qubein – I appreciate your words of wisdom. To the Source of all Wisdom, my Creator Jesus Christ, Your love is amazing and I am humbled by Your purpose for my life. –Keith

I want to thank my wife, **Helen** for being my best friend, my biggest fan, and the happiest person I know. I will love and cherish you forever! I also want to thank my children; **Kelsie** for her leadership and conviction, **Cale** for his character and sense of humor, **Clay** for his compassionate heart and zest for life, and **Kara** for her creativity and joyful spirit. Finally, I want to thank my parents, **David and Patti Hanson** for their example, their belief in me, and for a lifetime of joyful memories. –Doug

FOREWORD

This little book captures the essence of true success. It gives simple yet profound definitions of what it means to succeed.

Wise people realize that true success is a lot more than just money. The wisdom revealed in this book can empower you to not only succeed financially but also to create success in every area of life.

When this book uses the word success it is referring to having a sense of fulfillment, successful relationships, peace of mind, a healthy body, as well as financial freedom.

The principles revealed in this book not only create success but also significance. They give you practical insight of what to do and what not to do in order to succeed.

The definitions of failure revealed in this book give you an empowering perspective about failure. Failure, from a certain perspective, is a great teacher and has proven to be part of the path to success for some of the most successful people.

Wherever you are in the journey to success, the principles in this book will keep you focused on what's important. *101 Distinctions between Success and Failure* contains pearls of wisdom that are priceless. The insights in this little book can and will save you time, energy, and money in your journey to success, if you apply them.

Nido Qubein
President, High Point University
Chairman, Great Harvest Bread Company

DISTINCTION 1

Success is doing what you love.
Failure is doing what you hate.

Love makes you successful in every area of life. True success is being rich spiritually, emotionally, mentally, physically, and financially. Loving God makes you spiritually rich. Loving people makes you emotionally rich. Loving yourself makes you mentally and physically rich. And loving what you do to make money and what you can do for others with money makes you financially rich.

Most people are just getting *through* the day instead of getting *from* the day. Each morning we wake up and decide how we will invest our time. We literally trade in a day of our life to act on that decision.

Successful people are more often doing what they love than not. They look back with enthusiasm on how they lived today and are excited to pick up where they left off tomorrow.

Certainly, we all have to pay our dues from

time to time and endure a phase when we don't necessarily "love" our current situation. That doesn't mean we can't fill other parts of our day with something we do love.

Use your challenging times to serve you, instead of depress you. Get inspired to really think about your life and what you want. Develop a clear vision, in vivid detail of the life you desire and then take a small step every day toward that vision. You will "love" this process, regardless of your current circumstances, as your focus will shift from where you *are* to where you're *going*.

Success is doing what you love.

DISTINCTION 2

Success is living in abundance.
Failure is living in scarcity.

Abundance is your birthright. Everywhere you look in the universe, you see abundance. There is an abundance of people, animals, trees, stars, and galaxies. The only reason people live in scarcity is because they believe in it, which is to believe a lie. The truth is there is an abundance of everything you could ever want or need.

There is an abundance of love, peace, and joy. Yes, there are bad and evil things in the world but, if you look at the big picture, there are many good and beautiful things. What are you focusing on?

Focus on abundance and you will start to attract it into your life. People who become successful and fulfilled have an abundance mentality. People who struggle have a scarcity mentality. Your mentality determines your reality. Develop an abundance mentality. Believe there is more than enough for you and everyone else and you will be more successful.

Success is living in abundance.

DISTINCTION 3

Success is enjoying the present moment.
Failure is living in the past.

The present moment is what matters in being successful. When you concentrate on the present you will enjoy it more and you will accomplish more. Focusing too much on the past or the future takes away from the power of the present.

Don't spend your time regretting the past or worrying about the future. Learn from your past and plan your future, but give your greatest attention to what you are doing right now. If you live in the past, you will repeat it. If you worry about the future, you will create the things you are worrying about. If you take positive actions in the present moment, you will become successful and fulfilled.

The present moment is the only place you can experience peace. Fear of the future creates stress. Thinking about what you *woulda*, *shoulda*, or *coulda* done in the past creates regret. Live in the present and enjoy your life. Right now, this moment, you have countless things you could give thanks for. You have many people in your life who love you and would feel massive happiness if you expressed your love to them. Do it right now, and see how you feel.

Success is enjoying the present moment.

DISTINCTION 4

Success is having hope for the future.
Failure is fear of the future.

Hope is one of the greatest powers of life. A person with hope will persevere until he achieves his dreams. A person without hope is a person with fear. Fear will cause you to give up on your dreams.

Whether you are going to have hope for the future or live in fear of the future is your personal choice. Believe that good things will happen to you and through you, and they will. Believe that you are going to encounter problems and eventually fail, and you will.

Fear is a terrible darkness that blinds you to opportunities and the joys of life. Hope is a bright light that empowers you to see an abundance of opportunities and enjoy the best that life has to offer.

Success is having hope for the future.

DISTINCTION 5

Success is finding happiness where you are.

Failure is looking for happiness in the future.

Have you ever known someone who has everything by the world's standards, i.e., a gorgeous house, a beautiful spouse, good health and wealth; yet they are the unhappiest person you ever met? Likewise, have you ever known someone who has nothing by the world's standards and yet they always have a smile on their face? Happiness is nothing more than a choice, and it's something everyone has the ability to find, regardless of his or her current situation. For most people, happiness and success are something they are working for in the future; tomorrow's payoff for today's pain.

One of the challenges with setting goals is that some people misunderstand the purpose. Goals are essential in guiding your actions to reach your future life. But don't let the goal for something you want to be, do, or have in the future prevent you from enjoying the wonderful life you have right now. Wherever you are right now, there are thousands of people who would trade places with you if they could. There are people who long for the health you take for granted, your financial position, your job, your family, your popularity, your outlook, and your future.

Success is finding happiness where you are.

DISTINCTION 6

Success is peace of mind.
Failure is stress and worry.

Is there anything more precious and valuable than peace of mind? If there is, we don't know about it. Peace of mind empowers you to connect with the wisdom within you and to make right decisions.

Stress and worry are weaknesses and bring confusion into your life. Stress is a by-product of worry. I once heard *worry* defined as: "using your imagination negatively."

I think most people who study personal development buy into the timeless philosophy: "we become what we think about." Dreams are the result of using your imagination and thoughts correctly. Worry is nothing more than using this same power, your imagination, to create an undesirable circumstance in your mind. Stress develops as you live out the non-existent negative circumstance in complete detail, including all the consequences to your finances, relationships, and quality of life.

To make the right decisions that create success, you must have peace of mind. Having peace of mind, in and of itself, is a success; and it also creates more success.

I've found the easiest way to nurture peace of mind is to simply have faith. Faith that there is a higher source of power in control. Faith that all things happen for a reason.

This mindset allows me to let go and simply enjoy my life instead of trying to think through every detail and control every outcome.

Success is peace of mind.

DISTINCTION 7

Success is a focused mind.
Failure is a distracted mind.

Focus is power. When light is focused it becomes a laser that can cut through almost anything. When your mind is focused on what you want in life you can cut through almost anything that comes across your path. Knowing who you want to become and what you want to do and what you want to have in life is more powerful than any laser. Having a vivid vision, a definite direction, and a powerful purpose empowers you to live life to the fullest.

Success is not an accident. It is a planned outcome. Plan your successes and stay focused on them. Don't let other people or things distract or discourage you from your dreams. Decide what you want to be, do, and have and focus on it every day.

Success is achieved by those who focus. The more you focus on your goals, the more power you have to make them happen. The more you focus on your goals, the quicker they will be realized. As your life develops, your smaller successes will lead to bigger ones. You will gain momentum and confidence, and feel the joy that comes from personal growth and achievement.

Success is a focused mind.

DISTINCTION 8

Success is knowing.

Failure is doubting.

Most people doubt their power. To be successful, you must have confidence. You can't consistently doubt yourself and create success.

You have the power to learn and grow and do most anything you wish. If you are willing to learn the natural laws that govern our current time on earth, take action, apply what you learn from life's lessons, and persevere, you will create great success.

Whatever you want to do in life, know you can learn how to do it. Doubting that you can fulfill your dreams will guarantee you don't. You are more powerful than you realize. Believe, have faith, trust that you can, and you will.

All success starts with faith. All failure starts with doubt. When you choose to have faith, you begin to develop an inner knowing that is beyond description. Feed your faith and starve your doubts. A deep sense of knowing is power. Trust it, follow it, and find your success.

Success is knowing.

DISTINCTION 9

Success is taking action.

Failure is inaction.

We've all been told information is power. Actually, that's not true. Information is *potential* power. Real power comes from action.

Think about it. We all know what foods to eat, that we should exercise, and how to nurture healthy relationships. Bookstores and the Internet are full of information on how to make money, how to connect with your children, and how to lower your golf score. What distinguishes success-ful people is not *how much they know*, it's that they take *action* with what they know.

Action is the key to success. You can't sit around and wait for other people to make things happen for you. You must decide you are going to make things happen for yourself.

Countless numbers of people are waiting for their ships to come in—but they never even sent one out!

What are you doing right now, today, to move

you towards your dreams? You may not know *everything* you need to do, and you probably have a list of things you're certain would move you closer, but you haven't started.

Dreaming big dreams and using your imagination are important, though you will not experience success until you start taking action. If you're not living the life you want to live, then it's time to act. If you're taking action but not getting the results you want, then it's time to change your actions and do something different.

Whatever you do, don't just sit there and do nothing or you'll get nothing. If you don't know what to do, then educate yourself and apply your new knowledge. Wisdom is not the possession of knowledge; it is the application of knowledge. Wisdom leads to success.

Success is taking action.

DISTINCTION 10

Success is achieved with purpose.

Failure is achieved without purpose.

Why are you doing what you're doing? Why do you want to be successful? When you create a purpose for becoming successful, you will find success is achieved much easier and with more joy and excitement. You need a deeper meaning for wanting to become successful than a desire for success alone.

Success without a real purpose requires a *disciplined* approach. Discipline, which requires conscious thought, is always a short-term approach. Ultimately, your discipline will give way to your true desires, which work on a subconscious level.

A person who goes on a diet to lose weight with sheer willpower and discipline may lose weight but, in the long run, the true desires win and the weight returns. However, a person who has a long-term purpose for how they want to look and feel creates a new identity and the wrong lifestyle loses its appeal. Losing weight becomes effortless and keeping it off becomes a habit.

Do you want to have the freedom to spend more time with your family? Do you want to travel? Do you want to make a difference in people's lives? Most people would answer yes to those three questions and they are all great purposes to create success.

Be sure you have purposes for creating success and you will have a stronger motivation to take action and make things happen. If you are seeking success without purpose, you will struggle and eventually give up, which is ultimate failure.

Success is achieved with purpose.

DISTINCTION 11

Success is a choice and learned behavior.
Failure is just learned behavior.

People don't consciously choose to fail; though people who succeed consciously choose to succeed. We learn to fail from people who have tried something and given up and then tell us what we can or can't do. If you choose to become successful, you will have to learn new things and stop listening to what others tell you.

You must first choose to be successful, then you learn how to be successful. Learn to think differently. Choose to continually expand your mind and learn to look at things from different points of view. Choose to be around successful people. Choose to take risks. Choose to learn from your mistakes and try again.

Your life is a reflection of what you learn. Choose to do whatever it takes to be successful.

Success is a choice and learned behavior.

DISTINCTION 12

Success is keeping the main goal
the main goal.

Failure is not having a main goal.

It doesn't matter what your main goal is. What matters is that you have a main goal. You have purposes for each area of your life and there is probably one main lifelong purpose that you should be focusing on.

What is the one thing that inspires you the most? What would you love to spend your time doing? What are the deep desires of your heart? Your answers to these questions should be your main goal.

If you keep the main goal the main goal you will meet with success and fulfillment. Having a main goal gives you a target, something to aim at.

Having a main goal keeps you focused. Having a main goal is an absolute must to becoming successful and fulfilled. Did Martin Luther King Jr. have a main goal? What about Mother Teresa? Tiger Woods? Lance Armstrong? Bill Gates?

I believe the reason we are so captivated by the Olympics is because the athletes are so committed. No one in the Olympics is casual about his training or his event. They often trade four years of their lives to prepare for one competition. They wake up in the morning thinking about one thing, their main goal, the Olympics, and they prepare in every way possible.

After you've decided what your main goal is, you must keep it your main goal and not let other things take your attention away from it.

Success is keeping the main goal the main goal.

DISTINCTION 13

Success is having faith.

Failure is being afraid.

Having faith will lead you to the critical quality that all successful people have—the ability to take action. Fear will immobilize you. Part of having faith is believing good things are going to happen to you and through you. Being afraid is believing bad things will happen to you.

Whatever you believe, you will create the circumstances to confirm that belief. You will seek and find examples and situations that prove you are right. Be careful what you choose to believe because you will create it, even if it is based on a lie.

Faith is trust. Fear is doubt. Trust that good things are coming your way and you'll find they do. Doubt that good things are coming and you will find they don't. This may sound too simple, but in my experience it is absolutely the truth. It is often the simple truths in life that have the biggest impacts on people. Having faith and trusting in God, yourself, and others will always lead to success.

Success is having faith.

DISTINCTION 14

Success is the result of believing truth.
Failure is the result of believing lies.

Believing the truth leads to peace and prosperity. Believing lies leads to stress and poverty. In order to get the benefits of truth working for you, you must continuously seek and find truths.

Truth has benefits; lies have consequences. Success is a benefit of believing truth and failure is the consequence of believing lies. To find out if something is true, just do it and look at the results. If it produces positive results, it is probably true. If it produces negative results, it was probably a lie.

Failure that comes from believing lies can be turned into a success if you admit you were believing a lie and then look for the truth and change your belief. Failure is often part of the path to success because you find something that doesn't work, learn from it, and try again until you find the truth that gives you the results you want.

Truth creates life and lies destroy life. Seek and find the truth and you will be successful.

Success is the result of believing truth.

DISTINCTION 15

Success is the result of generosity.
Failure is the result of selfishness.

Being generous is a sure way to keep yourself on the path to success. Being selfish guarantees you will not find the path to success. The old saying, "You reap what you sow" could be summed up in two words: givers get.

Whatever you give away, you will get more of. If you give love, you will get love. If you are patient with people, people will be patient with you. If you give anger, you will get anger in return. If you are impatient with people, people will be impatient with you.

This also works in the area of money. If you give money away, you will get more money in return. Money is a form of energy and energy must keep moving. Being generous with your money will cause money to continuously flow to you and through you. Being selfish with your money will cause you to struggle financially.

Success is the result of generosity.

DISTINCTION 16

Success is walking in the light.

Failure is walking in darkness.

Walking in the light is knowing where you are going and why you are going there. Success is walking in spiritual light. Spiritual light reveals your life's purposes and makes your work more meaningful. Doing meaningful work is part of being successful.

Why do you do what you do? Having purpose and doing things that make a positive difference is like enjoying warm sunshine on your face.

Having no purpose is walking in the dark. Walking in darkness is not having a strong reason why you do what you do. Your life and work are not meaningful or fulfilling without purpose. To find your purpose and make your work more meaningful, ask yourself one simple question: what would make my life meaningful to me? Your answer is your spiritual light and will lead you to success if you pursue it.

Success is walking in the light.

DISTINCTION 17

Success is having vision.
Failure is being blind.

Vision is internal. Having vision for your life empowers you like nothing else can. Create a vision for where you want to be five, ten, even twenty years from now and focus on it. You will be amazed at the opportunities that come your way to help you get where you want to go.

First though, you must decide where you want to go. When you decide who you want to be, what you want to do, and what you want to have, then you will begin to understand what vision is all about.

Vision encompasses your whole life. It looks at the big picture and guides your thoughts and actions. What you can see and hold in your mind's eye can be created in this physical world. No one has ever done anything great without having vision. Without vision, you will fail. With vision, you will succeed.

Success is having vision.

DISTINCTION 18

Success is understanding.
Failure is confusion.

True understanding comes from experience. Take sports, for example. You can learn all the rules of football or golf from reading a book, but until you actually play the sport you won't really understand it. Success is like that. Until you take action with the knowledge you acquire from school, books, or other successful people, you don't understand what it means to be successful.

It is important to study success and it is even more important to take action with what you learn. I know people who think they understand business or real estate or stocks, but all they really have is knowledge. Until they open a business or invest in real estate or stocks they won't really understand.

To be successful, you must move from intellectual understanding to experiential under- standing. Experiential understanding comes from taking action. It is the result of real-world experience.

Success is understanding.

DISTINCTION 19

Success is taking responsibility.
Failure is avoiding responsibility.

Nido Qubein, the man who wrote the foreword to this book, came to the United States thirty years ago, when he was seventeen. He didn't speak a word of English. Today he is a multimillionaire, runs several companies, created a foundation responsible for raising and distributing millions of dollars annually for educational funding to America's youth, and is president of the very university he attended. How does someone accomplish so much with such a difficult beginning?

According to recent studies, immigrants who enter the United States are four times more likely to be financially successful than natural-born American citizens. How can this be?

Immigrants come to this country with a different perspective. They know they are in the land of opportunity and they take personal responsibility for their lives.

The more you take responsibility for your life, the more you can have. As long as you think your life is someone else's responsibility, you will be a victim and your success will be extremely limited. If you blame other people for your situation you will constantly struggle.

Blaming, complaining, and justifying are ways of avoiding responsibility. Taking responsibility means to give up blaming, complaining, and justifying.

It is within your power to change the results of your life. Your life situation is not someone else's fault. If you believe the lie that it is, you will remain weak and helpless. If you believe the truth—you have the power to create your life— you will become strong and successful.

Success is taking responsibility.

DISTINCTION 20

Success is being creative.

Failure is being reactive.

$\mathbf{Y}$ou have the power to create the life you want. If you don't believe this, you will find yourself always reacting to what other people say and do. Life doesn't just *happen* to you. Life *responds* to you.

The thoughts you have change how you feel. The way you feel affects the actions you take. Your actions dictate your results and your results give energy to your current direction. Positive results generate positive thoughts, and the cycle repeats itself.

Unfortunately, unless you are aware of this cycle, negative results can lead to negative thoughts and a negative cycle. Become aware of your thoughts and words. Consciously choose to think and talk about what you want and you will ultimately create it.

If you are reactive, you will spend your time thinking and talking about what you don't want, and you will create it. From one point of view, there are two types of people in the world, creative and reactive. From a higher perspective there is only one type of person in the world, and that is creative. You can choose to create peace and prosperity or you can choose to be reactive and experience stress and poverty. Either way you are creating your life.

Success is being creative.

DISTINCTION 21

Success is a noun.

Failure is a verb.

Success is something you are. Failure is something you do. You don't become successful by making a lot of money. You make a lot of money by becoming successful. Success is not determined by what you have, it is determined by who you are.

Failure is part of the path to success. Everyone who is successful has failed many times. You must never identify yourself as a failure. I repeat, failure is a verb, it is just something you do occasionally, not something you are.

You can make failure a noun by giving up. But, if you keep on keeping on and try again after you have failed, you are a success. Getting knocked down doesn't make you a failure, staying down does. If you view yourself as a failure, it is time to pick yourself up and realize you are one step closer to success. Success is something you are, not something you do.

Success is a noun.

DISTINCTION 22

Success is keeping your word.
Failure is breaking your word.

Integrity is an absolute must. Successful people value their reputations and make sure they keep their word. If there is ever a doubt in your mind as to whether you will be able to keep a promise, don't make it. It would be better to disappoint someone by being honest than to lie and lose their respect by breaking your word.

People who develop a reputation of honesty are able to build long-lasting personal and business relationships. It is impossible to build meaningful relationships if people believe you will break your word. Trusting relationships are not established quickly, they are developed over time. Every time you keep your word you gain momentum and are entrusted with more. Every time you over-promise and under-deliver, you lose momentum and are entrusted with less. Keeping your word is always important. It will make you successful. Breaking your word will lead to failure.

Success is keeping your word.

DISTINCTION 23

Success is the result of wisdom.
Failure is the result of foolishness.

Wisdom creates success while foolishness creates failure. Wisdom is simply making the right decisions and foolishness is making the wrong decisions. The decisions you make on a daily basis lead you to success or failure. Even small, seemingly insignificant, decisions can have major consequences in the long run.

We all know what we should be doing, but most of us don't do it. Wisdom is deciding to apply our knowledge. It is taking action on what we know is right.

Financially speaking, if you decide to spend everything you make and not save and invest, you will eventually be a financial failure. Physically speaking, if you always eat junk food and never exercise, you will eventually have heart failure. On the other hand, if you decide to save and invest, you will become a financial success. If you eat healthier and exercise regularly, you will be strong and healthy.

Wisdom is making decisions consistent with what you want most. Foolishness is trading what you want most for what you want now. Wisdom makes decisions that create success. Foolishness makes decisions that create failure.

Success is the result of wisdom.

DISTINCTION 24

Success is the application of knowledge.
Failure is the application of ignorance.

Knowledge is based on truth, facts, and information. Ignorance is the result of lies, rumors, and lack of awareness. Applying the truth in any area of life will create success in that area. Applying ignorance in any area of life will create failure. Truth creates peace and prosperity; lies create stress and poverty.

In order to have knowledge, you must pursue it. Knowledge does not come to an idle mind or body. Knowledge takes effort: reading books, personal experiences, listening to wise people, asking great questions, and diligent thought.

Ignorance is a by-product of laziness and arrogance. Have you ever considered how much you spend each year on your car? Take a moment to add up the payments, maintenance, gas, insurance, regular cleaning, and all the accessories for one year. Next consider how much you spent on your mind last year. If you spent more on your car than you did on your mind, you need to re-think your strategy. Your mind will take you places your car never will. Without the proper knowledge, your only option will be to act on ignorance.

Successful people embrace lifelong learning and enlightened action. Ignorant people are satisfied with what they already know and do the same thing over and over, hoping for a different result.

Success is the application of knowledge.

DISTINCTION 25

Success is knowing who you are.
Failure is doubting who you are.

Who are you? You are a free spirit, not a trapped soul. You are a human being, not a human doing. You are not your actions. You are not your thoughts and feelings. You are not a victim. You are so much deeper and stronger than these.

The more you become aware of how powerful you are, the more success you will experience.

What are your gifts? Most people don't think they have any gifts. Does that mean God made a mistake when he made you? I don't think so! We all have gifts, and we also have one other important birthright—we get to choose what we do with our gifts! We can choose to do nothing with them or do everything.

Can you imagine if Michelangelo chose not to paint? What if Pavarotti chose not to sing? Who else could do the things that were put inside of these people? No one.

The same is true for you. If you don't sing your song, it will never be sung. Only you can sing your song!

First, you must *choose* to identify your gifts. Maybe you are gifted in music, math, or art. Maybe you have the ability to make complex subjects easy or the ability to inspire people to take action. Maybe your sense of humor is your gift, or your ability to raise money for charitable causes. Recognize your gifts and then use them. Success is sure to follow.

Success is knowing who you are.

DISTINCTION 26

Success is to appreciate.

Failure is to complain.

Appreciation is powerful. When something appreciates it rises in value. When you appreciate your life, your life will become more valuable to you.

I believe that whatever you appreciate, you get more of. If you appreciate money, you get more money. If you appreciate love and respect, you get more love and respect.

I also have the same belief about complaining, which reminds me not to do it. Whatever you complain about, you get more of. Complaining is talking about things you don't want or like. The problem with complaining about something is you continue to get more of it. If you complain about not having enough money, you will continue not having enough money. If you complain about being stressed, you will continue being stressed. Complaining causes you to remain the same. Appreciation causes you to grow.

Success is appreciation.

DISTINCTION 27

Success is having deep and meaningful relationships.

Failure is being lonely.

One of the most important and fulfilling things in life are deep and meaningful relationships. It has been said that if you have more than five close friends, you can consider yourself fortunate.

There is no amount of money or any possession that can replace having a strong circle of friends. When you are on your deathbed, you will not be concerned with the money or things you acquired. You will be concerned about the people you have relationships with. Don't wait until it's too late. Give and receive love, patience, kindness, joy and forgiveness now. Focus on building meaningful relationships with your family and friends.

It is impossible to truly enjoy life without someone to share it with. Give people the attention they deserve. Encourage them to strive for their goals. Support them in pursuit of their dreams.

Success is having deep and meaningful relationships.

DISTINCTION 28

Success is trusting others.

Failure is suspecting others' intentions.

Trusting others is a sure way to get their respect. It is also a way to show others respect.

The journey of success requires a team. You will always need help with something. This book is a collaborative effort between two authors and a variety of other people behind the scenes. Trusting one another not only made this book happen, it made it better and more fun to write.

If you are constantly suspicious of people, it will keep your success extremely limited because people can sense when you don't trust them. Nobody likes it when someone else questions their intentions. Do you? Of course not, so don't do it to others. Most everyone is doing the best they know how to do. When you learn to let go and trust people your relationships will get stronger and your success will expand. I have found that trusting people makes them better persons and they do better jobs.

Success is trusting others.

DISTINCTION 29

Success is following your heart.

Failure is being driven by your ego.

I heard EGO stands for "Edging God Out." Have you ever been driven by your ego? At times, we all have, and it is usually when we are stressed and fearful.

Your ego has no power to give you peace. Following your heart gives you peace and leads you to success. Your heart understands things that are beyond your ego's ability to grasp. Your heart trusts others and has faith that things will work out. Your ego will always be afraid something bad is going to happen. Your ego is fearful and selfish. Your heart wants to love and serve.

Remember the first distinction in this book. Success is doing what you love. Learn to listen to your heart, have the courage to take action, and you will succeed. Your heart won't give up, your ego will. Don't let your ego run your life or you will always be stressed and full of fear.

Success is following your heart.

DISTINCTION 30

Success is playing full-out.
Failure is being checked out.

Successful people play full-out. They are energized, creative, and fun. Failures, on the other hand, look for ways to do as little as possible. They are checked out and only happy when they cause other people to check out with them.

Failures are lethargic, stagnant, and frustrating to work with. Have you ever worked with someone who is checked out? Someone who is just getting through the day? They bring down the whole team, don't they?

There is nothing more exciting than working alongside someone who has a can-do attitude; someone who values you and the experience the two of you are creating. Successful people look for ways to do more than what is expected of them.

Think about your approach to your job, marriage, and community. How would people describe your attitude and effort? Are you getting *through* the day or are you getting *from* the day?

Success is playing full-out.

DISTINCTION 31

Success is complimenting.

Failure is competing.

A sincere compliment is the most powerful way to connect with another person. Everyone wants to feel significant and be recognized for their skills, actions, and personal qualities.

Successful people know that true success is never achieved alone. Ultimately other people must be involved in your endeavors. Every person you meet is a potential customer, supplier, investor, partner, employee, or advertiser. If you make an effort to recognize their qualities, they will do the same for you.

One of the laws of the universe is when you give, you receive. Failure results when we see others as a threat and choose to compete with them. If we see someone as a threat, we unconsciously move from a healthy mindset to a fearful one, and often react in a malicious manner.

Gossip, lies, and manipulation can become a

way of life when we are in a fearful competitive state. This road is dark and lonely and leads to bitterness, unhappiness, and anger.

Always take the higher road. Find something good in at least one person every day and give them a surprise compliment. By the end of one year, you will have given 365 compliments and, I think, you'll find that you have received many more.

Success is complimenting.

DISTINCTION 32

Success is having more than enough.
Failure is not having enough.

You might wonder why you would need more than enough. The answer is, so you can do good for others. People who have just enough for themselves approach life from a place of scarcity and are powerless to help others in their times of need.

Set your goals higher than just surviving. Set your sights on abundance—so you can help others with your surplus. A survival mentality will cause you to have barely enough. When your reason for wanting a lot more is bigger than your own needs you will see opportunities that you were once blind to.

There are plenty of opportunities around. The people who see them and profit from them want more than enough. If you worry about not having enough, you will be unable to see opportunities that are in front of you.

Aim to have more than enough and let part of the reason be so that you can help others.

Success is having more than enough.

DISTINCTION 33

Success is realizing you don't
know much.

Failure is thinking you know a lot.

Humility makes you rich; arrogance
makes you poor. There is so much to know about
life and success that it is complete nonsense to
think you know a lot. An arrogant attitude keeps
you from looking at things from different points of
view. It keeps you from growing.

A humble heart causes you to seek and find
things you didn't know so you can become richer.
If you realize you don't know much, then you are
able to learn. If you think you know a lot, it will
keep you from acquiring more knowledge. There
is always another level of life you can go to, but it
requires you to learn something new to get there.

Walk in humility and keep looking for new
things. Beware of the words "I already know
that;" they keep you stuck where you are.
Whatever you think you already know, you can
know it better.

Being humble empowers you to gain a deeper understanding of things you think you already know.

Success is realizing you don't know much.

DISTINCTION 34

Success is believing in your dreams.
Failure is doubting yourself.

Dreams are funny, they can excite us and scare us to death all at the same time. Whether you make your dreams come true or not depends on whether you focus more on the fear or the excitement of achieving your dream.

Do you believe in your dreams or do you doubt yourself? Doubt is a relative of fear. When you doubt yourself, fear keeps you from taking action. Proof that you believe in your dreams is the actions you take towards achieving them. If you're not taking actions towards your dreams, then you may be letting fear stop you.

Success is acting in spite of your fear. People who don't quit realize dreams. If you have given up on your dreams, it's not too late to believe again and go for it. Dreams don't have deadlines. Dare to believe in your dreams and start taking action today.

Success is believing in your dreams.

DISTINCTION 35

Success is finding the good in all things.
Failure is finding the bad in all things.

Have you ever noticed children seem to be happy most of the time? Children can turn a cardboard box into the best toy they've ever had.

Kids also have the ability to forgive and forget. If Mom or Dad reacts too harshly to a situation and later apologizes to the child, the child forgives and forgets almost immediately, like it never happened.

As we get older, we tend to lose such qualities. Instead, we begin to find the bad in all things and we develop a photographic memory towards those we care about most, documenting in detail every mistake they've ever made.

Think about this. If you had five great experiences today and one slightly negative event, which are you most likely to focus on? For most people, it's the negative one. I've noticed as people age and experience more of life's disappointments, they tend to grow cynical and negative. Ironically, they also experience more joy and happiness, but they tend to forget those or take them for granted.

To break this cycle, we have to raise our level of awareness and change our philosophy. I subscribe to a philosophy I learned from a good friend: "nothing is good or bad until I choose." This empowers and challenges me to find the good in all situations. It takes courage to adopt such a philosophy because it's not always easy, but it's worth it.

Success is finding the good in all things.

DISTINCTION 36

Success is taking the high road.

Failure is taking the easy road.

Success is not an easy journey. If it were, more people would be successful. Unfortunately, most people are more interested in a comfortable destination than an exciting journey, so they take the easy road. The easy road is lined with businesses and activities that appeal to the easy crowd: bars where people can drink their problems away, parties where people can gather to gossip and complain, and shops where people can spend their money on items of indulgence.

The high road is lined with businesses and activities that improve the mind, body, and spirit, like universities, churches, libraries, health clubs, and foundations where people make a difference in the lives of those less fortunate.

People on the easy road tend to complain, blame, and call people names. They tend to be unhappy, stressed, and lost on their journey through life. People on the high road tend to compliment, forgive, and find the good in people. They tend to be happy, at peace, and clear about their priorities in life.

The high road is not necessarily *for* everyone, although it is accessible *to* everyone. It is a difficult road to reach, and even more difficult to navigate. It requires a different level of thinking and a higher degree of skill.

The easy road has few rules. You can basically react to your impulses and do whatever you want, while expecting others to adapt to your behavior. The high road, however, requires personal responsibility and has many laws that must be obeyed, such as integrity, love, appreciation, forgiveness, patience, kindness, peace, goodness, faithfulness, and contribution.

What road are you on right now? It is easy to get swept up with the crowd and travel down the easy road. Taking the high road is nothing more than a conscious decision to live at a higher standard than the masses.

Success is taking the high road.

DISTINCTION 37

Success is being confident.

Failure is a lack of confidence.

One main reason people fail is a lack of confidence. And most people lack confidence because they focus on their failures more than their successes. Successful people fail too, but they have the ability to forget about them and move on.

Baseball players fail 70 percent of the time at the plate. Football's greatest quarterbacks fail more than 40 percent of the time with their pass attempts. Pro-basketball players make only half of their shots, and professional actors and actresses are turned down on average 29 of 30 times when auditioning for movie roles.

There are several ways to develop self-confidence, which is a process that takes time. One is to set yourself up to win. Most people establish unrealistic goals and therefore feel defeated too often. If you're dieting, give yourself a goal for tomorrow that you know you can achieve. Build the muscle of discipline and get a little tougher on yourself with each success.

Another strategy for confidence building is to simply think back to a time in your life when you were self-confident. A time when you were on a roll! Play some music that will help inspire you, close your eyes, and relive what it was like to feel totally confident, and then open your eyes with the assurance that you still have that person inside of you.

A third way to build your confidence is to start trying new things. It's difficult to develop the confidence necessary to become successful without trying new things. I know people who have a hard time doing anything new because of negative childhood or early adult experiences. Regardless how you were treated as a child, at some point in your life, you have to choose to reject the opinions of others and believe in yourself.

Confidence is believing in yourself. It's normal to want and even need others to believe in you, but they never will until you believe in yourself.

Success is being confident.

DISTINCTION 38

Success is a journey and a destination.
Failure is just part of the journey
to success.

The most precious aspect of success is the process. Reaching your definition of success is a wonderful feeling, but the ups and downs of the journey are priceless because they help define who you are. Real success is not measured by what you have, it is who you have become.

Ultimately, your riches and results will not be what you value most. Instead you will cherish the stories you enjoy sharing with others and the relationships you developed on your journey. Setting your eyes on a successful lifestyle will cause your life journey to be one powerful lesson after another. These lessons prepare you for success by making you a better, stronger, and wiser person.

The journey of success sometimes includes necessary failures. Unfortunately, most people endure the difficult times with agony, only to look back years later on a challenge and say, "That was

the best thing that could have happened to me."
Why wait until later to come to that conclusion?
Consider your life right now and mentally trans-
form your tragedies into triumphs. What
challenges or failures have you experienced
recently? What have you learned from these setbacks and how are they preparing you for future
success? If you learn the lessons that life is trying
to teach you, you will enjoy the process and arrive
at the destination of success.

Success is a journey and a destination.

DISTINCTION 39

Success is to be thankful.

Failure is to take people and things for granted.

Having gratitude is one of the easiest ways to experience success. Being thankful for the people in your life is a deep and powerful way to feel good. There is always something you can find about others that you don't like, but there is usually something you can be thankful about as well. Look for the good in others and it is much easier to be thankful for them. I believe people can sense when you truly appreciate them. They can also sense when you take them for granted.

People who feel like they are being taken for granted don't usually remain with you for long. This goes for a spouse, a child, or an employee. If you want deep and meaningful relationships, then be more thankful for the people in your life.

This goes for things also. If you want to enjoy success, you must appreciate everything you have or you may end up losing it.

Success is being thankful.

DISTINCTION 40

Success is having health and wealth.

Failure is gaining wealth while losing health.

There is an old saying that there are people who lose their health while they pursue wealth, then, after they have wealth, they would gladly give it all back to have their health return. I think you would agree that is a foolish way to live.

It is a worthy goal to pursue financial freedom but not at the expense of losing your health. Go ahead and set big financial goals, but make sure you give priority to your physical health. When you focus on health and wealth your life is much more balanced and you are able to enjoy your wealth a lot more.

I knew a man who worked hard until he was in his early sixties. He was very successful in the furniture business and decided to retire and move to another state to be near his daughter and new grandchild. Unfortunately he had not taken good care of his body, and only two years after retiring he died. He worked hard his whole life and only had two years with his family before passing on. Don't let that be you. Take care of yourself. Don't lose your health while gaining wealth.

Success is having health and wealth.

DISTINCTION 41

Success is communicating your
best feelings.

Failure is communicating your
worst feelings.

Every relationship has challenges. We are such complex creatures there is no way we can always see everything eye-to-eye. Since we are spiritual beings, we have a desire to connect and be at harmony with everything in the universe. However, we are also emotional creatures with strong desires to fully express ourselves. Successful people understand this conflict and behave differently than unsuccessful people.

It is healthy to express your true feelings, but it causes problems if you say hurtful things you don't really mean. Meaningful communication is almost impossible when you are angry or hurt. Learning to calm down and wait until you are in a peaceful state to address issues is wisdom.

How many divorces would have never happened if that advice was followed? How many business partnerships would still be going strong today if people hadn't said things they didn't really mean?

You are able to connect with your true feelings when you are at peace. When you are stressed or angry is not the time to try to have a heart-to-heart. The danger in saying things you don't really mean is that once you say them, you feel obligated to stick with them. Most people feel the need to be true to their words, even when their words are not really what they wanted to say.

Success is communicating your best feelings.

DISTINCTION 42

Success is a planned outcome.

Failure is the result of not planning your life.

Success is not an accident. It is the result of planning. This is true in every area of your life. If you want successful relationships with your family, friends, and business associates, then you need to plan to spend time with them. If you want to be successful in having a strong and healthy body, then you need to plan your exercising. If you want to prosper financially, then you need a plan.

A simple way to express this important truth about success is: plan your work and work your plan. This simple discipline will keep you focused and create success quicker than you can imagine. I'll bet you have a plan for how to accomplish tasks at work. Do you have a plan for how to make your marriage work? A plan for your finances? What is your plan for health and vitality? If you do not plan your success, then you will react to every distraction that comes into your life. Not planning creates stress and uncertainty. Plan your life. Keep your plans flexible and expand-able. Planning is one of the most important parts of the success process.

Success is a planned outcome.

DISTINCTION 43

Success is a choice you must make every day.

Failure is letting others choose for you.

Placing your success in the hands of someone else is dangerous. It seems everyone is more than willing to tell you what you can or can't do, or what you should or shouldn't do with your life.

Your life, however, is your responsibility. If you want to be successful, and I know you do, then make the decision to do something every day to get closer to your goals. Letting others choose for you will almost certainly keep you from your goals.

In other words, if you don't have a plan for your life, you will become a part of someone else's plan. Why are you doing what you are currently doing? Is it what you really want to do with your life or is it something someone else has chosen for you? Does your current situation make you feel successful and fulfilled? If not, then it is time to start thinking about a change. If you find you need a change, start taking steps toward your aspirations with faith. Choose to do what you would enjoy doing.

Success is a choice you must make every day.

DISTINCTION 44

Success is finding and fulfilling your life's purposes.

Failure is not knowing your purpose.

Purpose leads to peace and prosperity. Not knowing your purposes ultimately results in stress and poverty. It is also important to realize you probably have one major lifelong purpose and several smaller *seasonal* purposes.

Seasonal purposes are critical in finding and achieving your major lifelong purpose. They are often overlooked as detours and roadblocks, but whatever you are currently involved in has a life lesson you must learn in order to get closer to your big dream.

Find and fulfill the smaller seasonal purposes of your life and your main lifelong purpose will be revealed to you. Pay attention to your circumstances to see what you can learn. One of the main purposes in life is to grow. Commit to personal growth and you will find you are on the path of purpose.

Success is finding and fulfilling your life's purposes.

DISTINCTION 45

Success is enjoyed more when shared.
Failure is not sharing your successes.

To enjoy success you must share it. Anything we share we are able to enjoy more. Being successful and not sharing it, is a miserable way to live. What good is it to have millions of dollars and not enrich others' lives?

Sharing intensifies human relationships and allows us to appreciate whatever it is we are sharing.

Whether it is money, time, happiness, or energy, we enjoy our lives more when we share.

Keeping your blessings and gifts to yourself is boring and unfulfilling. It is fun to share and celebrate with others. What are some of the successes you could share with others? What are some of your friends' and family's successes that you could acknowledge and celebrate with them? After you answer these questions, take action and see if life doesn't become more exciting.

Success is enjoyed more when shared.

DISTINCTION 46

Success is being able to hit a curveball.
Failure is always bailing out.

In order to hit a curveball you must have courage. Throwing a curveball is an effective pitch because of the fear it instills in the batter and because it requires different reactions based on how it's thrown. After letting the batter see a fast-ball or two, pitchers often come back with a curveball that starts on a path toward the batter's head.

The fear of getting hit by the pitch causes some batters to duck out of the way, only to feel foolish when the ball curves in for a strike. The next time the pitcher throws, he can start it off over the plate, where it looks like a strike. Batters are usually afraid of this approach as well, since a swing at this pitch usually results in an embarrassing gyration as he tries to reach a ball that is several feet out of his reach.

In order to be effective hitting a curveball, you have to read the spin on the ball, recognize the curve is coming, and then either have enough courage to stay in the box until it's time to swing or the discipline to lay off what appears initially to be a good opportunity.

Sometimes life throws curveballs at us. There are always going to be issues that arise to test who we are. Like in baseball, we have to be able to recognize what is coming and then adapt our actions accordingly.

Sometimes you need courage to stick it out; sometimes you need discipline. Knowing to expect the unexpected is valuable knowledge. It helps you be ready for anything. If you want life to be in perfect order all the time, you are setting yourself up for disappointment.

Has life thrown some curveballs at you lately? What was your response? Did it make you want to quit, to bail out? Develop an attitude that whatever comes your way today, you can handle. Just using the term "curveball" instead of "problem" is a good start. Be prepared for the unexpected.

Success is being able to hit a curveball.

DISTINCTION 47

Success is the result of positive habits.
Failure is the result of negative habits.

People are creatures of habit. Positive habits make you successful; negative habits cause you to fail. It doesn't get much simpler than that. Whatever you want to accomplish in life will require you to develop the proper habits to get it done.

A habit is part of who you are. Developing new habits requires a lot of discipline in the beginning. Notice I said "in the beginning." The wonderful thing about discipline is that it is only discipline until it becomes a habit. Once a behavior becomes a habit, it's no longer hard to do. It becomes automatic.

The most common way to develop a habit is through repetition. Set up a system where you are reminded to think or act differently than you have in the past. Studies have shown that after about twenty-one days of repetition, most actions become habit.

Your chance for success is greatly increased if you also write down your motivation for the new desired behavior. This helps your brain get a handle on the pain/pleasure trade-off: the painful consequences of continuing with your old habits and the pleasure you'll experience when you change. Pay the price of discipline and you will reap the reward of a positive habit.

Discipline yourself to start doing what you need to do and stop doing that which holds you back. Work hard to develop positive habits and they will make you rich.

Success is the result of positive habits.

DISTINCTION 48

Success is a benefit of discipline.
Failure is a consequence of laziness.

Discipline reaps benefits and laziness has consequences. Positive habits are some of the greatest benefits of discipline. Negative habits are some of the worst consequences of laziness.

Discipline also gives you self-confidence. Laziness causes you to doubt yourself. You can achieve whatever you want if you are willing to discipline yourself to get it. If you are lazy you will never achieve what you want.

Discipline leads to victory and laziness causes you to be a victim. Discipline shows you have self-control. Laziness will cause you to be controlled by others. People who are disciplined are super achievers. People who are lazy reap the consequence of regret. A lazy person says, "I should have, I could have, I would have, but I didn't." A disciplined person says, "I did."

Success is a benefit of discipline.

DISTINCTION 49

Success is paying the price.

Failure is wanting something for nothing.

Are you willing to pay the price for success? Wanting something for nothing is wishful thinking. To have successful relationships you must invest time in them. To be healthy you must invest time exercising. To become more successful you must continue to invest in knowledge.

Notice I use the word *invest*. I don't spend my time, energy, and money; I invest them into the things I want. If you want to be healthy, you must pay the price. If you want good relationships, you must pay the price. If you want more money, you must pay the price.

Investing your time, energy, and money into what is important to you is paying the price. If you spend your time, energy, and money doing things that don't fulfill you, then don't expect the life you truly desire to magically appear one day. It doesn't work that way. Pay the price to get what you want.

Success is paying the price.

DISTINCTION 50

Success is walking your talk.
Failure is when you don't walk your talk.

Have you ever known someone who always talked about what he was going to do but never did it? I imagine he didn't have much respect in your eyes. We must be careful not to do this ourselves. Such behavior not only diminishes our standing with others, it also affects our self-esteem.

Don't go around blabbing about what you are going to do. Do it first and then talk about it. People respect action and results, not talk and hype. Trying to impress people with your plans is not nearly as impressive as your results.

You should have a group of people you can talk with about your ideas, a group that will support and encourage you. But, outside of this group, don't try to impress others with what you're going to do. Do it first and then share the news. Telling others what you're going to do and then not doing it makes you a failure in their eyes.

Success is walking your talk.

DISTINCTION 51

Success is being rich in every area of life.

Failure is improving one area of your life at the expense of another.

True success is more than just financial abundance. True success is about balance. It is balancing your spiritual, emotional, mental, physical, and financial lives.

What good is a million dollars if your health is bad? What good is a million dollars if you are stressed out of your mind? What good is a million dollars if you don't have deep and meaningful relationships or feel a close connection to your Creator?

In order to be rich in every area of life you must consciously choose to be. You must have a desired outcome for each of the critical components of your life and you must put regular thought into how to get there.

Don't focus too much on money but don't neglect it either. Give sufficient time and energy to each area. Don't neglect your finances, family, friends, yourself, your body, or your Creator. Learn to be rich financially as well as spiritually, emotionally, mentally, and physically.

Success is being rich in every area of life.

DISTINCTION 52

Success is leaving a legacy.

Failure is leaving nothing for the next generation.

Do you have plans to leave a legacy? How will you be remembered when you are no longer here? What will live on after you are gone? Who will cry when you die? These are important questions to consider. Most people have a deep desire to pass on something of value to future generations. If you are one of those people, I suggest you start taking action today for what you will leave behind tomorrow.

Influence your family with love, patience, kindness, and forgiveness. Your example is one of the most powerful things you can leave as a legacy. The knowledge and insights you have gleaned over the years are valuable pieces of yourself that you should pass down to future generations.

An easy way to leave a legacy is to journal your life. You will be amazed how you've grown when you read older journals. Dreams that once seemed out of reach are part of your normal day. Things that once left you fearful are now easy. You will learn from your journals; and your family, for generations to come, will find nuggets of hope and wisdom from your life.

You could also consider your financial legacy. Have you ever considered setting a goal for how much money you would like to pass on to your family and the charities you believe in?

Success is leaving a legacy.

DISTINCTION 53

Success is a benefit of having the right friends.

Failure is a consequence of having the wrong friends.

Building the right relationships, with the right people, at the right times in your life is critical to being successful. It is also important to realize that some of your friendships will be temporary. Trying to hold onto a relationship that you should let go of will only hold you back.

Make the effort to build relationships with people who have achieved the kinds of success you want to achieve. You are apt to become like the people you associate with on a regular basis, so take a close look at the people you spend most of your time with. Do you want to be like them? If you answered yes, that's great. If you answered no, then it is time to find the right friends. The wrong friends will keep you from living up to your potential. The right friends will encourage and inspire you to become the best you can possibly be.

Success is a benefit of having the right friends.

DISTINCTION 54

Success is following your heart.
Failure is following your flesh.

Your heart dreams big. It tells you to do something special with your life and not to be like everyone else. Your flesh tells you not to reach for the stars; you could be hurt. Be like everyone else.

Following your heart takes courage. It's exciting to pursue the things that really inspire you. You were created to enjoy your life and the truest and deepest joy you can experience is found when you follow your heart.

It is impossible to be bored when following your heart. Being bored is a sign you are simply surviving, a characteristic of following the desires of the flesh. Remember, everyone dies, but not everyone truly lives. Be one of the few people who live their life with purpose. Think of something you've always wanted to do and take one action today towards making that desire a reality.

Success is following your heart.

DISTINCTION 55

Success is being internally motivated.
Failure is being externally controlled.

When you are internally motivated you have a clearly defined and understood "compelling reason why." To know *what* you want is exciting; to know *why* you want it is powerful. Unfortunately, many people are externally motivated; they seek incentives and trinkets for their efforts. They will not feel truly successful until they are internally motivated.

To be internally motivated you must have a vision for your life that is bigger than you. If you are only focused on yourself, someone or something else is probably externally controlling you. Only focusing on you is a selfish and fearful way to live. When you are selfish and fearful other people can manipulate you into doing what they want you to do. When you have a big vision that encompasses a lot more people than just yourself you will be internally motivated to fulfill it and that keeps you from being controlled by others.

Success is being internally motivated.

DISTINCTION 56

Success is achieved by trying new things.
Failure is the result of doing the same
old things.

What kind of results are you getting in your life? It is foolish to keep doing the same old things and expect new results. If the results of your life are not what you want, then it is time to try something new. Sometimes when we plan on trying new things, we are met with fear. Fear of the unknown, fear of failure, fear of rejection. One of the keys to success is acting in spite of your fears.

Don't let fear stop you. Fear is always worse in your mind than in reality. Shine the light of faith into the darkness of fear and the fear will disappear.

Faith is action. When you take action and try something new, your fears disappear. Fear doesn't leave you alone until you take action. Be aware that you may face fear when you think of trying something, but take action anyway. Do something different and you will get new results. If you want something you've never had, you must do something you've never done.

Success is trying new things.

DISTINCTION 57

Success is working for profits and wages.
Failure is working for wages only.

Financial success is achieved quicker and easier by working for both profits and wages. You can make a living by working for wages but you can make a fortune working for profits. Focus on both.

Have something you do that secures your lifestyle and also take risks that could give you some great rewards. If you're only concerned with security, your success will be limited and you may end up a financial failure.

Life rewards those who take risks. Find something, a product or service, that you can buy for one price and sell for a higher price. Put your attention on making profits and you're much more likely to be a financial success.

People who make millions have multiple sources of income and, therefore, work for profits and wages. People who struggle financially work for wages only.

Success is working for profits and wages.

DISTINCTION 58

Success is enjoying the seasons of life.
Failure is not realizing life has seasons.

Just as there are natural seasons that
govern our physical world, there are supernatural
seasons that govern our lives. The natural seasons
have much to teach us about the supernatural.
Take farming, for instance. In the spring farmers
plant seeds; in the summer they work the soil,
keeping everything watered and free of weeds; in
the fall they reap a harvest; and in the winter they
rest. These four natural seasons contain wisdom
for our supernatural seasons.

Our lives aren't comprised of one cycle of the
seasons. We can have many summers and springs
in our lives, as well as multiple winters and falls.
What season are you in right now?

During the springs of our lives we should take
action, think ahead and make plans for our future.
In the summers of our lives we should be working
hard on our plans. In the falls of our lives we
should be receiving the benefits of our hard work

and celebrating our successes. In the winters of our lives we should take time to rest and recover, reflecting on the past to gain wisdom, knowing that another spring is around the corner.

Just like farmers, we can't rush the seasons through their cycles. And just like farmers have faith that nature will ultimately provide what they need, so should we. This is wisdom for all aspects of our lives; spiritually, emotionally, mentally, physically, and financially.

Success is enjoying the seasons of life.

DISTINCTION 59

Success is fulfilling the deep desires of your heart.

Failure is seeking to fulfill the deceptive desires of your mind.

The deep desires of your heart are what you would love to do with your life. They inspire you. The deceptive desires of your mind are the lies you believe about what you can or can't do based on the beliefs and expectations of other people. People who experience success and fulfillment seek to fulfill the deep desires of their hearts.

Your deep desires are your purposes—what you were created to do. They lead to peace and prosperity. Your deceptive desires are the things you have been conditioned to believe will make you happy. Deceptive desires are society's standards, not yours, and are, therefore, instinctively received by your subconscious as lies. Your deep desires are purely yours and, therefore, received as truth.

Learn to discern between the deep desires of your heart and the deceptive desires of your mind.

Success is fulfilling the deep desires of your heart.

DISTINCTION 60

Success is being goal driven.
Failure is being indulgence driven.

People with goals achieve success much sooner than people without goals. In fact, people without goals don't usually succeed at all. They get distracted looking for anything that will quickly make them feel good, and often turn to excessive indulgences like excessive eating, drugs, alcohol, cigarettes, spending money, watching TV, playing video games, etc. for immediate gratification.

Having a goal gives you a target and will force you to use your time more wisely. Having a goal gives you a destination of where you want to go. With goals, your life has more meaning and purpose. People with goals get to where they are going because they have a destination. People without goals don't know where they are going and end up wandering around aimlessly. Having goals to pursue gives you a reason to get up and work every day.

What are your goals and what are the indulgences you could eliminate or reduce in order to help you succeed? If you don't have any goals, I challenge you to take time today to write some down. Set goals for every area of your life and commit to making them happen. Read over your goals every day and your life will become more exciting and fun. Eliminate your indulgences the same way you developed them, in small steps. Watch thirty minutes less TV per night, for example, and use that time to take action on your goals.

Success is being goal driven.

DISTINCTION 61

Success is laughing at yourself.
Failure is taking yourself too seriously.

A sense of humor is a great asset, especially humor towards yourself. Taking yourself too seriously removes the joy from your life. If you learn to laugh at yourself, you will make pleasant memories for you and your family. Laughing at yourself means admitting when you have goofed up. It means not getting angry when something doesn't go according to your plans. It means smiling more often so you feel peace and joy.

Taking yourself too seriously robs your life of energy. It makes it difficult to have meaningful relationships because you always feel like you must be right and someone else is wrong. Laughing at yourself means you are willing to be wrong and not care too much about what others think about you. When you can laugh at yourself you will find it much easier to attract good friends and your relationships become more rewarding.

Success is laughing at yourself.

DISTINCTION 62

Success is doing the best you can.

Failure is doing just enough to get by.

Doing the best you can increases your self-worth. You feel better about yourself when you go the extra mile. When you do the best you can, you work more efficiently and get more things done in less time.

Doing the best you can is energizing and inspiring. Doing just enough to get by results in boredom and sometimes depression. Doing just enough makes you think that life is boring. The truth is, life isn't boring, people are. People who do just enough to get by don't get much out of life because they don't put much into it.

Give life all you've got. Whatever you're involved in, do it with all your might. If you are working for someone else, work as if the business belonged to you.

Life rewards those who do the best they can. You never know who might be watching and might offer you a better opportunity if they see you doing the best you can. Even if no one is watching, still do the best you can, just because it's the right thing to do and it prepares you for more success.

Success is doing the best you can.

DISTINCTION 63

Success is having a dream that is worthy of you.

Failure is not having a dream.

Asking: "Am I worthy?" is the wrong question. The right questions are: "Are your dreams worthy of you? Are the things you are doing worth your time? Are you investing your time or are you spending your time?" These questions will help you focus on what's truly important to you.

We often get caught up doing things that are not fulfilling. That's why it is so important to have a dream that is worthy of you. Without a dream, you will waste your life. With a worthy dream you will invest your life in something of value.

True success is investing your life in something that makes a positive difference. Take the time to ponder the question: "What would make my life meaningful?" Your answer will be a worthy dream.

Success is having a dream that is worthy of you.

DISTINCTION 64

Success is creating win-win relationships.
Failure is creating win-lose relationships.

Your life is defined by your relationships. In other words, the quality of your life is directly linked to the kind of people in your life and the depth of your relationships with them.

Successful people understand this principle and are conscious that in order to get momentum in life, every relationship should lead to another relationship.

This is the basic concept of networking. You won't be able to develop a network of relationships if you are creating win-lose relationships. People that negotiate win-lose deals think they will be perceived as shrewd when they gain an upper hand. Later they wonder why people approach them with caution and suspicion, or worse, don't approach them at all.

Win-win relationships stem from an abundance mindset. Win-lose relationships stem from a scarcity mindset. Win-lose relationships are based on power and control. Win-win relationships are based on trust, long-term considerations, and mutual benefit.

Success is creating win-win relationships.

DISTINCTION 65

Success is learning from your mistakes.
Failure is repeating your mistakes.

Life always gives us new lessons to help us grow. Unfortunately we don't always learn a lesson the first time it is presented to us. If you pay attention to the lessons life sends your way and learn from them the first time, you will be amazed at how fast you achieve success.

I'm confident that right now you are experiencing a life lesson. What should you be learning from your current life lesson? People who ask this question on a regular basis enjoy a better quality of life. They learn from life and apply their new knowledge with better actions. Those that don't learn from their mistakes only complain and fail to change. It's as if they expect the universe to submit to their demands on how life should be.

Success is a process and there are some lessons we need to learn again and again, but it shouldn't be because we keep making the same mistakes.

When you make a mistake or something does

not go as you planned, you should immediately ask yourself "What is life trying to teach me here?" Come up with an answer and then change your actions and try again. Don't keep repeating the same mistakes. Try different approaches to whatever you are doing until you have learned the lesson that you needed to succeed.

Success is learning from your mistakes.

DISTINCTION 66

Success is expanding your mind.
Failure is closing your mind.

Expanding your mind is a wonderful habit to develop. It's also a lot of fun to see a bigger picture. To expand your mind, you must be willing to question what you believe.

Our thoughts are limited to our own experiences. We are limited by what we *think* we know. Expanding your mind is about seeking and finding new truths. If you want to make more money than you do now, you will need to expand your mind and learn something new.

Sometimes when you learn something new it will contradict what you previously believed. This is unsettling and causes many people to close their minds to the new information. In order for your mind to expand you must be willing to be wrong. A closed mind always defends its beliefs and perceptions. A closed mind would rather feel right about what it already believes than know the truth.

Many people get stuck at certain levels of life because they quit expanding their minds. There is always another level of life to go to, and arriving at a new level will require new information.

Success is expanding your mind.

DISTINCTION 67

Success is giving respect to others.

Failure is disrespecting others.

Respecting other people results in success. Disrespecting others is one of the surest ways to meet with failure. There have been millions, perhaps billions, of relationships ruined because one or both of the parties did not show respect to the other. A relationship that is built on respect will endure the tough times.

Showing respect is showing love. Being disrespectful shows you don't understand love. We have no right to disrespect anyone. We may not like something someone else does, but we should still show him or her respect.

One of the main reasons to respect others is because that's what we earn in return. And, of course, the reverse is true. Show disrespect and that's what you get in return. Think of someone in your life right now who you often share conflict or tension with. Do you show them respect? I would guess you don't. I would also guess that they don't show you much respect either. Find something they do that is good and let them know you respect them in that area. You might be surprised with what happens to your relationship. Regardless, taking the higher road will make you feel better.

Success is giving respect to others.

DISTINCTION 68

Success is a lifelong process.
Failure is finding your comfort level and staying there.

The process of success is never-ending. Throughout your life you can grow. This means you can continue to become more successful if you choose. The more you expand your vision, the richer and more fulfilling your life will become. If you allow the pleasure of your successes or the pain of your failures to cause you to stop growing, you will become discontent and unfulfilled.

No matter how successful you become, there is always another level you can attain. The human spirit needs to keep reaching for higher ground. It is easy to understand that you shouldn't let your failures stop you. It is more difficult to understand that your past successes can also be a hindrance to your growth. It is important to celebrate and enjoy your successes. It is also important to not let your successes make you so comfortable you stop growing.

Success is a lifelong process.

DISTINCTION 69

Success is being happy with yourself.
Failure is being upset with yourself.

Learning to be happy with yourself is a great achievement. (We are often our own worst critics.) Taking responsibility for your life does not mean you beat yourself down at every turn. The problem with being critical of yourself is that it can keep you from building up any momentum towards success.

If you work hard at a relationship or business, take the time to praise your efforts. Pat yourself on the back once in a while. Look in the mirror and remind yourself of all you do that is good.

It is a powerful practice to celebrate small successes. We often believe that unless we do something big or dramatic, then we haven't done anything important. Many times it is the small successes that make the big ones possible.

Look back at your life and find the small successes and be happy with yourself. You'll find that as you nurture yourself, you will begin building the confidence necessary to take on larger challenges. Don't compare yourself with others. That is a form of failure and can cause you to be upset with yourself.

Success is being happy with yourself.

DISTINCTION 70

Success is a lot more than just money.

Failure is a lot more than just a lack of money.

Have you ever wondered why money is commonly linked with the word *success*? There are many reasons for this association, including the security that comes with financial freedom, the lifestyle of wealthy people, and the unique experiences that people with money enjoy.

I also think money and success are directly linked because money is like a scoreboard. It's a tangible way of keeping track of who is the most "successful."

Deep down, however, we know this isn't the best way to determine success. We all know someone with plenty of money who is miserable. We would never want to trade places with them, no matter how much money they have.

Success is much more than money. Success is an overall balance of the key elements of life; things like mental awareness, physical health, emotional maturity, spiritual connection, social interaction, family relationships, and financial strength. Likewise, failure is much more than just a lack of money. I've known many people in life with little or no money whom I admired, even modeled in my own life.

Wherever you are right now, you are probably enjoying success in one or more of the key elements of life. Build on those successes and keep growing in the other areas.

My relationship with God and my family are at the foundation of my definition of success. Nothing is more important to me than developing a relationship with God and honoring my family. In which areas are you currently enjoying a level of success and which ones are most important to you?

Success is a lot more than just money.

DISTINCTION 71

Success is persistence.

Failure is giving up.

Persistence is one of the keys to success and there is no substitute for it. If you know where you want to go and you don't give up, you will eventually get there. Giving up is not an option if you are committed to fulfilling your dreams. Those who give up, show that they weren't really committed in the first place.

Most people will persist until the going gets tough, then they give up. A few people will keep on keeping on until they reach their goals and these are the people who become successful. There is truth in the old saying "Tough times don't last but tough people do." Being persistent is being tough. It means you are committed to doing whatever it takes to be successful. Don't settle for less. That's called giving up, and you will feel like a failure when you do. Become a "whatever it takes" person and you will succeed.

Success is persistence.

DISTINCTION 72

Success is finding your voice.
Failure is not having a voice.

Everyone has a song they are destined to sing. And there are people who are destined to hear the songs we sing. The messages each of us were given to promote matter to those who need to hear them.

Your voice is your purpose. What is the message you are here to proclaim to the world? Find your voice and you will find your audience.

The world has millions of issues that need to be addressed. What angers you? What do you enjoy doing more than anything else? Your answers to these two questions may give you insight into the problems you are destined to solve.

Here is another approach. If you had a billion dollars, what would you do differently? What would you commit your life to? The truth is that whatever you answered, you can start making progress towards it now.

Success is finding your voice.

DISTINCTION 73

Success is living like you were dying.
Failure is dying without having lived.

If you knew you were going to die tomorrow, what would you do today? Is there someone you would call? What would you say? What are you waiting for? Living like you were dying is a powerful perspective on life. It helps you stay focused on what really matters.

When you reach the end of your life you are not going to wish you had spent more time at work. Imagine being one hundred years old, sitting in a rocking chair, and thinking back on your life. What would you like to have accomplished?

Each of us has a day marked on God's calendar that will be our last one here and our birthday in Heaven. Some people are wise enough to remember this every day.

It is true that everyone dies, but that doesn't mean everyone lives. It is sad so many people go through life just existing, but not really living.

Take some risks. Don't play it safe all the time. Live your life knowing that it is a short ride and you are here to enjoy it.

Success is living like you were dying.

DISTINCTION 74

Success is the reward of wisdom.

Failure is the consequence of foolishness.

To receive the rewards of wisdom you have to take risks. The bigger the risk you take, the bigger the reward you could receive. It is wise to take risks. This is not to say you shouldn't calculate possible losses. When you consider taking a risk, stop and ask yourself these three wise questions: What is the best that could happen? What is the worst that could happen? And, what is the most likely thing to happen? If you are inspired by the best, willing to deal with the worst, and if the most likely thing to happen gets you closer to your goal, then take the risk.

It is foolish to take risk without considering the consequences. Doing foolish things leads to being punished, not rewarded. Wisdom gives rewards. It is wise to consider the rewards as well as the consequences when taking risks.

Success is the reward of wisdom.

DISTINCTION 75

Success is overcoming your fears.
Failure is succumbing to your fears.

Fear is an illusion. It is the result of believing something to be true that is not true. Fears are based on lies. Most fear is a fear of something that might happen in the future, but since the future hasn't arrived yet, it can't be true. It is just a belief.

You have to be careful believing what will or will not happen in the future. If you have fear about the future, it is likely that your own thoughts will manifest your fears into reality.

Faith overcomes fear. Faith is trusting that good things will happen in the future. Faith leads to success and fear leads to failure. Overcome your fears with your faith.

Faith and fear are choices. Choose to have faith in the future and you will overcome your fears. If you feed your fears by thinking about them too much, you will fail. Feed your faith by trusting that things are going to work out for your good, and you will succeed.

Success is overcoming your fears.

DISTINCTION 76

Success is being immune to criticism and praise.

Failure is being affected by criticism and praise.

Everyone knows how criticism can damage self-esteem and negatively affect one's overall mindset; but only the wisest of men recognize that excessive praise can be equally destructive. Praise can inflate our egos and make us prideful. People with these characteristics seldom succeed because over time they take themselves too seriously. They don't listen well or treat others with respect.

Praise is a form of respect. Therefore, it makes sense that the person praising you deserves respect in return.

Being immune to both criticism and praise means you pay little attention to what others say about you. You alone need to decide who you are and who you want to become. Being affected by praise or criticism is to let other people decide who you are and who you are becoming.

Keep your heart humble. No matter how much success or failure you experience, it will serve you well not to pay too much attention to the praise or criticism of others.

Success is being immune to criticism and praise.

DISTINCTION 77

Success is freedom.
Failure is bondage.

You shall know the truth and the truth shall set you free. You can experience freedom when you apply truth in every area of life. Any area that you feel trapped in is a sign that you believe a lie, or lies. Lies take your freedom away and put you into bondage.

There are religious prisons, emotional prisons, mental prisons, physical prisons, and financial prisons. In order to get out of prison you must identify the lies that you believe, reject them, and choose to believe the truth, which is usually the opposite of the lies you identified.

Any time you feel trapped, stop and ask yourself what you are focused on and you will find that you are believing a lie. Believing lies puts you into bondage and believing the truth sets you free. The truth can hurt at times, but after it has done its work you will feel the freedom that you want.

Truth is light; lies are darkness. If you are used

to the dark, truth will hurt your inner eyes until you get used to the light. Then you will be able to see and be free. Seek and find the truth and you will find success.

Success is freedom.

DISTINCTION 78

Success is an ever-expanding vision.
Failure is narrow vision.

Never let your vision stagnate. Let your vision grow and expand into a life of its own. Create a vivid vision and let it be flexible enough to encompass new ideas and opportunities. You never know when a new idea might come along that will complement your vision and make success happen more quickly.

As you get close to seeing your vision fulfilled, start to increase it. It is a dangerous time in a person's life when they fulfill a vision, unless they expand their vision to encompass more.

Continuing to expand your vision ensures you will remain inspired and excited. Accomplishing a vision without expanding it can sometimes be a disappointment because the thing that inspired you for so long is now over. Make sure you have an ever-expanding vision and life will always be meaningful.

Success is an ever-expanding vision.

DISTINCTION 79

Success is being able to sit still
and be content.

Failure is rushing around all the time.

Hurry and worry will almost certainly result in failure. Few people can sit still and be content. Practice sitting still for twenty minutes without feeling anxious. When you can do this on a regular basis, you will find you are better prepared to face the challenges of daily life. Always running around and worrying about what might happen is a stressful way to live.

Learn to sit still and to focus your mind on what gives you peace. Peace and contentment need to be cultivated in your life in order to achieve real success. Set aside time each morning to create a peaceful state of mind; five minutes can help tremendously, but do twenty if you can. If you can't, then practice until you are able.

Carry that peaceful state into your day. If you find yourself getting stressed or worried, take time to refocus and get your peace back. Peace is power.

Success is being able to sit still and be content.

DISTINCTION 80

Success is peace and prosperity.

Failure is prosperity without peace.

Many of the distinctions I have already made between success and failure are reaffirmed with this one. Prosperity without peace is not true success. There is nothing more valuable than peace. Peace and prosperity are worthy goals, especially when you combine them.

Seeking peace without prosperity is only part of success, likewise so is seeking prosperity without peace. Don't seek one without the other. Seek and find both. They complement each other. Peace empowers you to create more prosperity.

When setting your goals to achieve peace and prosperity, give peace the priority and prosperity will follow. Peace is the foundation of true success. It is the foundation of lasting success. And it is the greatest asset you can pass on to future generations.

Success is peace and prosperity.

DISTINCTION 81

Success is being an optimist.
Failure is being a pessimist.

An optimist sees opportunity in every difficulty. A pessimist sees difficulty in every opportunity. An optimist views difficulties as challenges to be overcome. A pessimist views difficulties as reasons not to take action. Where an optimist finds a way, a pessimist finds an excuse. A pessimistic attitude doesn't do anyone any good. An optimistic attitude inspires others. An optimist believes there is always a way. A pessimist believes there is no way.

Most people forget that optimism and pessimism are both personal choices, not something genetically coded in your DNA or put upon you by an external force. You are not born an optimist or a pessimist. You become one or the other based on your conscious choices and your subconscious conditioning, i.e., self-talk, beliefs, and mental focus.

You must choose whether you are going to go

through life as an optimist or a pessimist. If you choose an optimistic attitude, you will create a successful lifestyle. If you choose to be pessimistic, you will play the role of a victim and constantly struggle. Success is achieved with the ability to spot and take action on opportunities that come your way. Optimism is power; pessimism is weakness.

Success is being an optimist.

DISTINCTION 82

Success is being awake.
Failure is being asleep.

Being awake is to behold the beauty of a sunset. It is watching an eagle fly. It is listening to the wind blow through the trees. It is taking time to enjoy the sweet smell of a flower. It is watching and listening to the ocean waves pound on the seashore. It is sensing summer metamorphose into fall.

There is so much beauty and mystery around, yet most people miss it because they are asleep. Living your life to the fullest means being awake to the beauty of everything around you. Someone who is asleep misses the magic of life. They are alive but they are not really living. Wake yourself up to the wonderful world you live in, enjoy the things that most people take for granted, and you will be a success.

Success is being awake.

DISTINCTION 83

Success is a calm spirit.

Failure is a worried soul.

People with a calm spirit are powerful. They overcome the problems of life with peace. Like water off a duck's back, the circumstances of life don't penetrate their inner worlds. A calm spirit is the result of a conscious choice to be at peace. A calm spirit accepts people and things as they are. A calm spirit doesn't react to bad news with fear and worry.

Any time you worry, you are flirting with failure. A person with a worried soul is weak and unable to handle the circumstances of life. Worry is weakness. Peace is strength.

A calm spirit is the result of trusting that the events of your life are meant for your good. A calm spirit comes from a belief that whatever comes your way today, you will learn from it and be better for it. A calm spirit is the friend of wisdom. When you are at peace you have the ability to make the right decisions.

Success is a calm spirit.

DISTINCTION 84

Success is the result of a burning desire.
Failure is the result of a weak desire.

In order to succeed you must, I repeat, must, have a burning desire. People don't become successful with a weak desire. The desire for success can be likened to fire. Fire consumes. The desire for success must consume you before you will ever attain it.

The thought that something must be consumed in order to obtain success is empowering. The success process will consume your time and energy. It will also consume your mind. If your time, energy, and thoughts are not being consumed with success, then you do not yet have a burning desire for it and you will not achieve it.

Make no mistake; success in every area of life is a worthy desire. It is much better to let thoughts of success consume you rather than thoughts of fear, stress, and worry. And it is much better to be consumed with the activities that lead to success than to lie around the house letting life pass by.

Success is the result of a burning desire.

DISTINCTION 85

Success is a loving relationship.
Failure is not having one.

A loving relationship makes you truly rich. If you have one, then you know what I am talking about. If you don't have one, then you probably want one. Here's a secret most people don't know about having a loving relationship: a loving relationship is not as much about finding the right person as it is about becoming the right person. If you understand this, then you have the power you need to develop a loving relationship.

If you think there is someone out there who is going to be perfect for you and you for them, think again. Loving relationships take work; they don't just happen. The work required to build a loving relationship is working on yourself. As you work on becoming the right person, you are much more likely to find and develop a loving relationship that lasts.

Success is a loving relationship.

DISTINCTION 86

Success is maintaining a sense of humor.
Failure is losing your sense of humor.

People who have a sense of humor have an advantage over those who don't. When you learn to laugh at life, you don't struggle so much. You take things in stride and know how to roll with the punches. People love to be around someone who can make them laugh, and nothing brightens a gathering more than a funny story that everyone can relate to.

Start looking for what is funny in your life. When situations arise, ask yourself what is funny about this. If you lost your sense of humor, it may require some effort to find it, but when you do, life will become fun again. An old man once told me, "We don't stop laughing because we grow old, we grow old because we stop laughing." Isn't that true? Learn to laugh at yourself and life. It will keep you young and full of positive energy. A friendly reminder though, don't laugh *at* people, laugh *with* them.

Success is maintaining a sense of humor.

DISTINCTION 87

Success is having meaningful work.
Failure is doing monotonous work.

There is nothing worse than doing monotonous work day after day after day. Work that is not meaningful can drive a person insane. People were created with a need to contribute and do things that give them a sense of fulfillment.

Sure, there are some things about daily life that seem to be monotonous. A great truth, though, is we can choose to create a positive meaning with almost anything in our lives, even taking out the trash.

If you are currently doing things that are monotonous on an ongoing basis, consider creating a positive meaning around them. Martin Luther King, Jr. once said, "All labor that uplifts humanity has dignity and importance and should be undertaken with painstaking excellence." Oftentimes when people define their work as monotonous it's them, not their job, that lacks enthusiasm. Whatever you do, do it with excellence. If you can't create a positive meaning around the work you do, then stop doing it and find something that makes your life meaningful.

Success is having meaningful work.

DISTINCTION 88

Success is pleasurable.

Failure is painful.

People want to be successful because they want pleasure. Everyone wants to feel good, so why don't more people become successful? Why is the pain of failure so widespread?

While there are many answers, I believe one of the main reasons is fear. When you fear something it usually comes to pass. Most people agree with the principle that your consistent thoughts create your current results. Think how fear can work against you. Fear leads to worry, and worry is nothing more than consistently thinking negative thoughts about how your life or a situation could play out. Therefore, your fears and subsequent negative thoughts manifest into reality the very things you are trying to avoid.

Success, on the other hand, brings pleasure and success is achieved with faith. Faith leads to peace and positive thoughts. Faith and fear are enemies. They fight against each other in making you succeed or fail.

If you want to consistently experience the pleasure of success, keep a clear vision of what success is for you, take action every day towards it, and have faith that it will come to pass when it's time.

Believe and trust that good things are going to happen to you. Failure and pain are the results of fear. Success and pleasure are the results of faith.

Success is pleasurable.

DISTINCTION 89

Success is admired.

Failure is despised.

When you are successful you automatically gain the admiration of many people. In fact, this is what motivates some people to achieve success.

Is it right to want the admiration of others? It depends on your motivation for wanting it. To desire admiration for reasons of personal significance or superiority is an ego-driven and misguided ambition. If you seek admiration so you can connect with more people and work together to make the world a better place, then your desires are honorable.

Let's face it, people listen to successful people. Energy attracts more energy. If you are successful, other successful people will want to know you, they will be more open to your ideas, and they will be more likely to be involved in your ventures.

Successful people help other successful people connect with each other, and their combined talents and efforts make a difference in people's lives. On the other hand, people who continually fail in life with unethical business practices, addictions, vindictive relationships, and poor values are avoided by the achievers. Be inspired to be successful so you can connect with the right people and make a difference in your corner of the world.

Success is admired.

DISTINCTION 90

Success is spending time with your loved ones.

Failure is to neglect your loved ones.

There is a balance between working to provide for your loved ones and personally being there for them. Success is finding that balance. Don't neglect your loved ones for the pursuit of financial gain.

Many people work hard to provide a better lifestyle for their families. Even though it is natural to want to provide the best you possibly can for your loved ones, you must make sure you are spending adequate time with them. Financial success and physical comforts are no substitutes for quality time with your family. People don't need more comfort; they need more love. Spending time with your loved ones proves your love to them.

Close, intimate relationships take time to build. Invest time in your relationships and your overall success will be deeper and richer.

Success is spending time with your loved ones.

DISTINCTION 91

Success is stretching your beliefs about what is possible.

Failure is letting your current beliefs define what is possible.

If you never challenge what you are capable of, you'll never know how far you can go. Your current beliefs have gotten you to where you are, but they won't take you any further. Letting your current beliefs define your future limits your success. It also causes you to fall behind those who stretch themselves and their possibilities.

Learn to ask yourself "what if" questions. Use your imagination and have fun dreaming. Take time to expand your mind. When you come up with a new idea, have faith in it and take some action. Ancient script says "All things are possible to those who believe." When stretching your beliefs, use your faith. Believe you can do whatever you set your mind to. Stretching your beliefs will inevitably lead you to new opportunities. When an opportunity presents itself, have faith and go for it. Don't keep doing the same old things or you'll always have the same old things.

Success is stretching your beliefs of what is possible.

DISTINCTION 92

Success is taking responsibility.
Failure is blaming someone else.

Blame is always about the past, which can't be changed. Taking responsibility focuses on the future. Taking responsibility for your life means you accept that you are in control of your life. Blaming others shows you believe you don't have control.

Whatever you believe, you will find evidence to support it, so be careful. Believe you are in control of your life, because you are. You can't control every event that happens to you, but you can control your thoughts, your feelings, and your actions. Realize that if you blame someone else for something, you have just given up your power to do anything about it.

Choose to focus on what you can do about situations instead of blaming others for things you don't like. Success is finding a way, not finding an excuse. Blaming is an excuse to give up. When you take responsibility you are being powerful, when you blame you are being weak.

151

Do you have an area in your life where blame has been your normal response? If so, try taking responsibility instead. What could you have done to avoid the situation? What did you learn from it? How are you a better person for it and how will you handle the situation differently in the future? Take responsibility for your life and create it the way you want it to be.

Success is taking responsibility.

DISTINCTION 93

Success is using time wisely.
Failure is being casual with your time.

You were given two resources at birth; time and your mind. How you use these resources will define your results. Successful people fully understand the value of their time. They know what every minute is worth and they prioritize their actions so they spend more time on important matters.

Failures don't think about the best use of their time. Instead they spend their day reacting to one crisis after another and wonder why they never seem to have time to make progress on their dreams. They complain that despite working all day, they never seem to get anything done.

Successful people are usually time fanatics and know the fundamentals of time management. They are able to run multiple companies, sit on several boards, be involved in charities, and still spend significant time with their families.

Each moment that passes in your life can never

be replaced. Start off each day by considering your dreams, your goals, and your legacy; then scan your to-do list and prioritize your actions to make the best use of your time.

This book is a result of this process. We had a million things that could distract us from writing, but none of them would help us reach our goal. So, now you hold it in your hands! Make the same progress in your life, on your dreams.

Success is using time wisely.

DISTINCTION 94

Success is going the extra mile.
Failure is doing just enough.

Someone once said, "It's never crowded on the extra mile." The reason is because few people go the extra mile. Most people give up too soon. One reason so few people are truly successful is because most people do just enough to get by. I have a saying that illustrates what happens to people who are doing just enough in their jobs: "People who do just enough not to get fired, usually get paid just enough not to quit, and nothing more."

Going the extra mile makes you more competent and builds your confidence. Going the extra mile prepares you for more opportunities. It separates you from the crowd and brings awareness to your abilities.

Doing just enough makes you like everyone else. Doing just enough keeps you from seeing new opportunities and causes you to settle for less.

Going the extra mile is paying the price of success. There are valuable life lessons that can only be learned on the extra mile. People who go the extra mile are able to create more success and they live with more fulfillment. Don't be one of the many, be one of the few.

Success is going the extra mile.

DISTINCTION 95

Success is dreaming big.
Failure is dreaming small.

If you're going to dream, you might as well dream big. It doesn't cost any more to dream big than it does to dream small. It takes the same amount of mental energy for either one. Dreaming small or not dreaming at all is to waste your mental energy.

We all have a need to feel like what we are doing is making a difference. Let's make sure that need is met by doing something that makes a big difference.

It is hard to dream big if your brain keeps asking, "How do I do that?" Obviously, you don't know how or you would probably already be doing it. Since you don't know how right now, your fears, specifically fear of failure and fear of the unknown, begin to influence you away from further consideration or taking action. Ultimately, you slip back into the life you already know how to live.

Here's the key component to dreaming big: don't worry about how. Focus more on *what* and *why*. Get really clear on what you want to do and why you want to do it. If you get a strong enough *what* and *why*, the *how* will come to you.

Whatever your dreams currently are, I challenge you to expand them and dream bigger. Dream in vivid detail about what your life will be like when you get there. You will probably be amazed at the unexplainable relationships that develop and the opportunities that begin to surface when you get this kind of clarity.

Success is dreaming big.

DISTINCTION 96

Success is keeping your dreams alive.
Failure is letting your dreams die.

Dreams don't have deadlines. I repeat: dreams don't have deadlines. If there was a time in your life when you had a dream, a goal, a purpose, or something meaningful you wanted to do, you can still do it. Don't let your dreams die with you, for that would, indeed, be a failure.

Success is believing in your dreams enough to never give up on them. Keep your dreams alive by thinking about them often; making plans; and, most importantly, by acting on them. Even small actions will keep your dreams alive. In fact, many dreams are achieved by doing a little bit every day towards them. Yes, do a little bit every day and you will find that it won't be long until you are much closer to your dream coming true. However big your dreams are, or were, you can get to where you want to go as long as you don't let them die.

Success is keeping your dreams alive.

DISTINCTION 97

Success is action toward what you want most.

Failure is action toward what you want now.

Failure is trading what you want most for what you want now. All of us will experience one of two kinds of pain in our lives, either the pain of discipline or the pain of regret. We can't escape both.

Either you will experience the short-term pain of discipline as you work to achieve your dreams, or you will experience the long-term pain of regret as you look back on lost time and opportunities.

Everyone has something or several things they want most. Maybe you want to be in a certain kind of physical shape or achieve a certain level of financial savings. Maybe you want to learn specific skills or have a vision for the perfect marriage. Whatever it is you want, you have to be willing to sacrifice what you want *now* for what you want *most*. You can't be in great shape if you give in to the temptations for unhealthy food and the comfort of lying on the couch instead of exercising. You can't have money for investing if you spend all that you earn, and you can't have the perfect relationship if you are not sensitive to your spouse's needs.

What disciplines are you engaged in that are important for your future and what temptations should you be aware of that are keeping you from the success you desire?

Success is acting on what you want most.

DISTINCTION 98

Success is having some fun every day.
Failure is being serious all the time.

Having fun every day is the best way to live life. Fun is defined differently for each of us, so it's important you know what would bring you happiness today—and then make it happen.

We all need something to look forward to. Remember when you were a kid and you were going to summer camp the next day? You could hardly sleep the night before, in anticipation of the fun week ahead. Even though you only got a few hours of sleep, when your parents woke you up, you sprang out of bed, eyes wide open, full of energy, and ready to seize the day! Compare that to how you woke up for an ordinary day of school. If you were like most kids, your parents had to drag you out of bed.

What is the main reason for the different energy levels? It's the fun you associated with the coming day. We are no different as adults. We need something to look forward to.

I've found that most people don't create fun in their day. Instead, they are waiting for something or someone fun to appear. How could you bring some fun into your life today? Tomorrow? This week?

If you're having trouble thinking of something, then you've probably been taking yourself a little too seriously. Think about what fun means to you and make sure you build in some things to look forward to every day.

Success is having some fun every day.

DISTINCTION 99

Success is exciting.

Failure is boring.

If your life is exciting, it's because you are exciting. You have energy, inspire others, and are doing things that are exciting. On the surface your life is simply a reflection of who you are inside. If you are bored with your life, you should look to yourself first. How are you growing? Are you learning any new skills? Trying new things?

One of the reasons people get bored is because they are looking for other people to add some excitement to their lives or to tell them what to do. In order to be successful, you must be passionate about your future. You cannot be passionate unless you decide for yourself what you want and what is important to you. No one can decide for you what is important to you.

Once you have this clarity, the journey is always exciting, even when there are setbacks. Boredom is the result of failure to make your own decisions. It's boring because you are taking action on someone else's plan, not your plan. Continually ask yourself, "What do I want in my life? What inspires me? What excites me?" Then take action to do those things.

Don't look to others to tell you what you can be, do, or have in life. Stop looking outside yourself for excitement, and instead follow your heart. Your journey to success will be exciting.

Success is exciting.

DISTINCTION 100

Success is improving your life.

Failure is staying the same.

The only constant in life is change. Change is inevitable; progress is not. Are you improving or staying the same? As the world changes, are you growing? One of the main purposes of life is to grow. Growing gives you a sense of fulfillment. People can make more money and not grow. Personal growth is real improvement.

Seek to improve in every area of your life. Increase your peace of mind; develop deeper relationships; get and stay physically fit; make more money; and, most importantly, stay connected to your source. Look at where you are today compared to five or ten years ago. Have you improved? Take inventory of how you've changed for the better and how your life's improvements mirror your personal improvements. Also take inventory of areas you could continue to do better in.

I have found that journaling my life is the best way to capture and understand how far I've come.

It is enlightening to read some of my past thoughts and compare them to the type of life I was living at the time. Scarcity thoughts were accompanied by a fearful and unhappy life. Healthy thoughts, filled with abundance and faith, were consistent with robust relationships and successful endeavors.

Success is improving your life.

DISTINCTION 101

Success is expressing your gifts and talents.
Failure is not using your gifts and talents.

Everyone has gifts and talents. Finding and using your gifts and talents leads to happiness and success. The best way to discover your gifts is to simply recognize what you have always been able to do easily; things that other people have always complimented you for, but you felt were nothing special. These are your gifts!

Maybe you are a great storyteller, excellent in math, funny, musically gifted, or able to manage large projects. Maybe you make complex subjects understandable, are good at creating systems and processes, or are skilled at building relationships. Whatever your gifts are, you probably take them for granted because you were probably taught that life is supposed to be hard. Maybe you were told that if you want to get ahead in life, you have to work hard. Therefore, anything that is easy for you must be of little value.

The truth is, the things that have always been easy for you are your gifts, and they are extremely valuable. Your gifts are the key to finding joy and success in your life. You will be most happy when you are doing what you love to do. Spend some time this week identifying your gifts and then begin trying new ways to use them in your life and career. It will bring significance and success to your life, and will glorify your Creator.

Success is expressing your gifts and talents.

ABOUT THE AUTHORS

Doug Hanson is nationally and internationally recognized as a speaker, consultant, and peak performance coach with customers in the United States, United Kingdom, Spain, Canada, Mexico, and Singapore.

Prior to being a speaker and consultant, Doug started his business career as a show director for ESPN televised sporting events. In the 1990s Doug worked for nine years in the computer industry as an enterprise sales and marketing professional for Toshiba, Texas Instruments, and Hewlett Packard, earning top sales honors seven times. During the Internet boom, Doug was on the original team that started bamboo.com, a leading-edge marketing company that grew to be the largest provider of online video content in just two years.

For seven years Doug was a featured facilitator at Tony Robbins' Life Mastery University in Hawaii. And in 2004, Doug was sought out by the NFL to address and energize the 6,000 volunteers involved in Super Bowl 38 at the pre-game rally held in Houston's Reliant Stadium two weeks prior to the big game.

In 1994, Doug created his company and committed his life to helping people find happiness and helping organizations develop a winning culture by improving their mindset, energy, skills, and connection.

Today, Doug lives in Katy, Texas, with his bride of more than twenty years and their four children.

Doug holds a bachelor's degree in computer science from Sam Houston State University and an MBA from the University of Houston, where he graduated with honors.

Keith Cameron Smith is a successful entrepreneur, best-selling author, and inspirational teacher. He is the creator of the Wisdom Creates Freedom Workshop that he teaches in businesses and churches around the country. He is also the author of The Top Ten Distinctions between Millionaires and the Middle Class—a powerful book that reveals the key distinctions that empower people to become financially free.

Keith has gained his success education through many successes and failures of his own, as well as from personal mentors who are some of the most successful people on the planet.

For five years Keith hosted his own radio show, "Flames of Truth," where he daily inspired thousands of listeners to pursue their dreams and become rich in every area of their lives. He is committed to teaching people how to strengthen their faith, increase their inner peace, and become totally financially free.

Keith lives in Ormond Beach, Florida, with his wife, Angie, and their two children.

For more information and to receive a free bonus, please visit our Website(s):

101distinctions.com

keithcameronsmith.com

doughanson.com